Gabrielle Bradshaw

Illustrated by
Gabrielle Bradshaw
and Michael Bradshaw

D0988051

A Magnet Book

First published 1989
by Magnet Paperbacks
Michelin House, 81 Fulham Road, London SW3 6RB
Text copyright © 1989 Gabrielle Bradshaw
Illustrations copyright © 1989
Gabrielle Bradshaw and Michael Bradshaw

ISBN 0 416 13832 2

Printed and bound in Great Britain by
Cox & Wyman Ltd, Reading

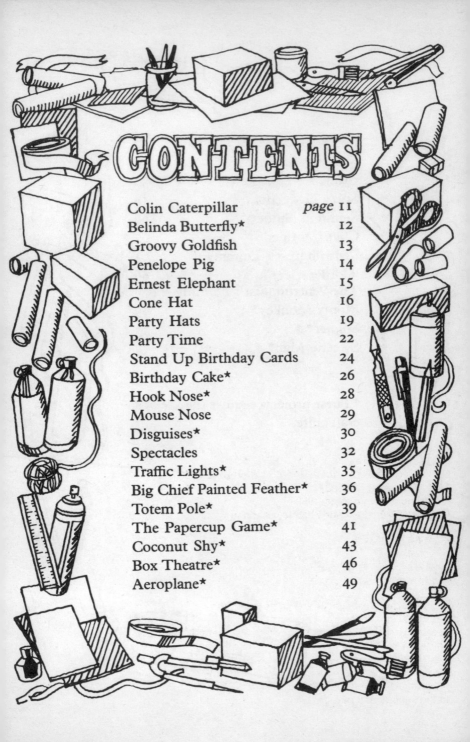

CONTENTS

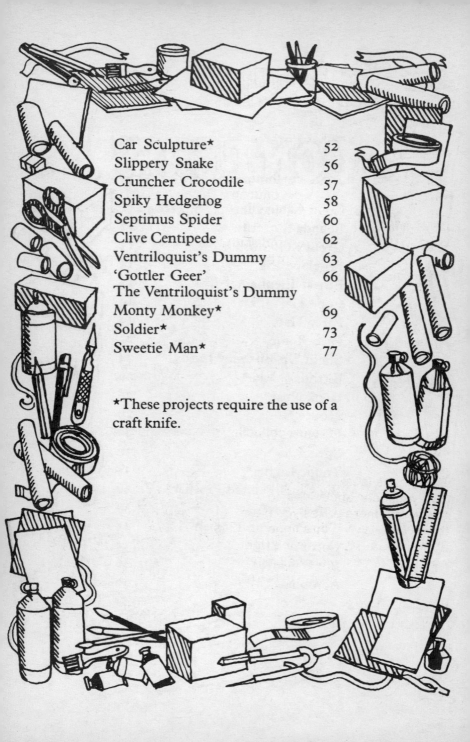

★These projects require the use of a craft knife.

INTRODUCTION

This book is about making things for fun: a disguise; a hat; a car a totem pole; or even a coconut shy. Once you get the hang of it you can make absolutely anything you like out of cardboard, paint and a little imagination.

Painters paint pictures and sculptors make objects. With a bit of practice and hopefully a lot of fun you can become a master sculptor in cardboard.

CARDBOARD BOXES AND KITCHEN ROLLS

It is a good idea to have a collection of boxes and rolls assembled before you start.

The shapes themselves will give you ideas about what to make. The more boxes you have the more likely you are to be able to choose one 'just the right size'. It is amazing how quickly you can get a collection of boxes

together. Supermarkets and shops are often glad to get rid of them, and parcels that come in the post often come in sturdy and interestingly shaped boxes. Ask everyone to save you their kitchen rolls, so that you always have material available to use.

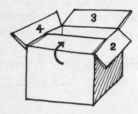

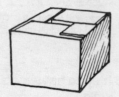

Most of the boxes are used as 'cube' shapes and unless otherwise stated should have the flaps on the open side folded in on themselves.

Fold the flaps down as shown. When you get to flap 4, tuck the last corner under flap 1. Put this side to the back or the bottom of the sculpture.

HOLES

Holes are another great way of joining shapes. They are useful when joining a kitchen roll to a box. Hold the kitchen roll up to the box and draw round it (A). The circle will of course be very slightly larger than the roll (B).

The object of this join is to get the roll to 'wedge' firmly into place. The hole therefore has to be cut just inside the drawn line (C).

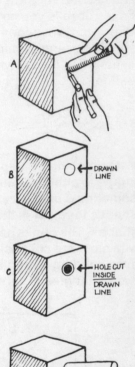

A

B ← DRAWN LINE

C ← HOLE CUT INSIDE DRAWN LINE

Push the end of the roll into the hole. It should be a tight fit and stay put (D). If the hole is too big the roll will fall out on to the floor. If the hole is too small the end of the roll will get crushed. The Sweetie Man's nose (see page 77), a triangular chocolate box works the same way.

If you want to make a tiny hole into card, maybe to start a cut or to thread through some elastic, you will need a very sharp pencil and a small lump of plasticine. Put the plasticine on a table and push the pencil through the card into the plasticine. This is the safest way to make a hole.

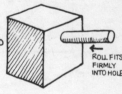

D ← ROLL FITS FIRMLY INTO HOLE

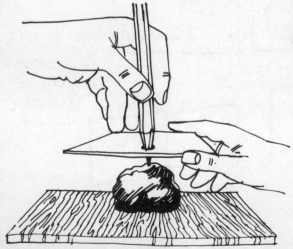

MEASUREMENTS

I have used very few measurements in this book. The size of the boxes or rolls you have will often dictate the size of the sculpture. Use your own judgement to decide how long or short something should be, and remember your sculpture doesn't have to look exactly like the drawing. The more personal you can make it the better.

SLOTS

When making a sculpture, one of the trickiest parts is joining one shape to another. Glue takes ages to dry and tape, although sometimes useful, can look ugly and is not always efficient. Slotting shapes together is the most effective way I have found for joining shapes. The join is neat and very strong. Also, sculptures made with slots are collapsible and can be taken to pieces for storing or even sending through the post. Practice the slotting technique on two rectangles of card.

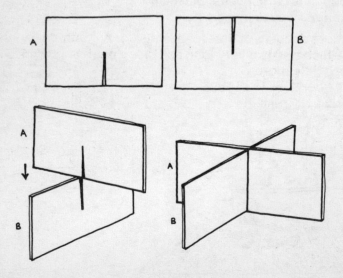

Cut a slot halfway up one rectangle in the centre (A) and halfway down the other (B). Lift up the first rectangle and slot into the second. The easiest way to cut a slot is to make two cuts into the card with a pair of scisors, making a very narrow triangle.

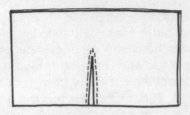

If you are not sure about the length and width of a slot, take it slowly. You can always increase it, until it is just right, but once you have made the slot too big, the join will become floppy and weak.

CARD

I only refer to two thicknesses of card. Medium-thick and thick. When I say medium-thick, I mean about the thickness of a cereal box. You could use cereal boxes to make some of the smaller sculptures, Groovy Goldfish (see page 13) for example. You can however buy sheets of this thickness fairly cheaply. A sheet of card gives you more scope with size, especially for something like the centipede which needs a very long body (see page 62). Thick card is of course a little more expensive. Whenever I can I cut up large boxes and use the sides.

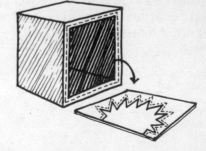

SCISSORS & KNIVES

Scissors are fine for cutting medium-thick card, but it is a lot easier to cut slots and holes into boxes and thick card with a craft knife. Some of you will be too young to use knives by yourselves. I am sure a parent or an older friend will help you. For those of you using knives, always treat them with respect. Always use a craft knife with a retractable blade and remember to close it down when not using it. Always direct the cut away from your body. Never leave knives lying around. The thicker the box the harder it will be to cut, it is probably easier to ask an adult to help with box slots and holes. At the beginning of each sculpture I have stated whether you will need a knife, scissors or both.

PAINT

A cardboard box can be transformed with a colourful coat of paint. Watery paint will give disappointing results. It will fade when dry. Strong vibrant colours are best. I use ready-mixed water base paints. This is easy to obtain. It comes in large squeezy bottles. The colours mix well, and you do not have to add water.
Do not be afraid of paint, use it thickly and generously. Also always allow plenty of time for paint to dry.

COLIN CATERPILLAR

We all know that caterpillars turn into moths and butterflies. Here's how to make a caterpillar and a butterfly using the same materials.

What you need:
One sheet medium-thick card. Cardboard rolls. Scissors. Paint.

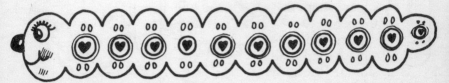

What you do:
Draw the caterpillar's body on to card and cut out. The body is made up of a head and lots of segments. You can make a caterpillar as large and as long as you like. Cut cardboard roll into sections about 4cm long.

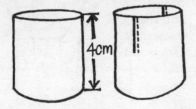

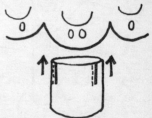

The sections are the caterpillar's 'legs'. Cut a slot halfway down either side of each section. Push legs up into the underside of body. Space 'legs' out all down the body. Paint brightly. Have a look at pictures of real caterpillars to get ideas about patterns and colours.

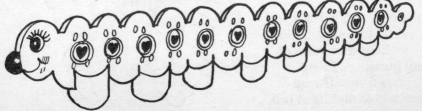

Belinda Butterfly

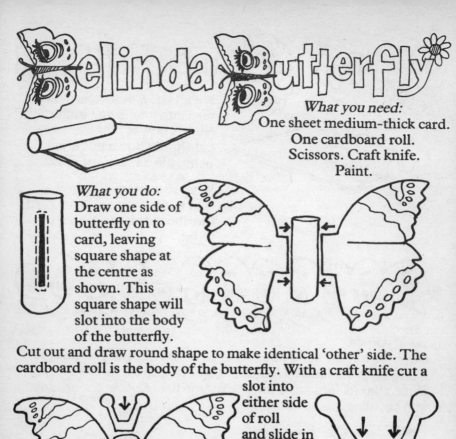

What you need:
One sheet medium-thick card.
One cardboard roll.
Scissors. Craft knife.
Paint.

What you do:
Draw one side of butterfly on to card, leaving square shape at the centre as shown. This square shape will slot into the body of the butterfly.

Cut out and draw round shape to make identical 'other' side. The cardboard roll is the body of the butterfly. With a craft knife cut a slot into either side of roll and slide in the wings. Draw and

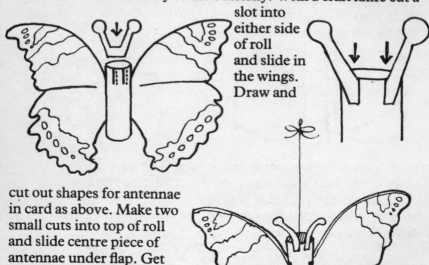

cut out shapes for antennae in card as above. Make two small cuts into top of roll and slide centre piece of antennae under flap. Get ideas for colouring Belinda by looking at pictures of real butteflies. Hang Belinda from a thread attached to middle of roll.

GROOVY GOLDFISH

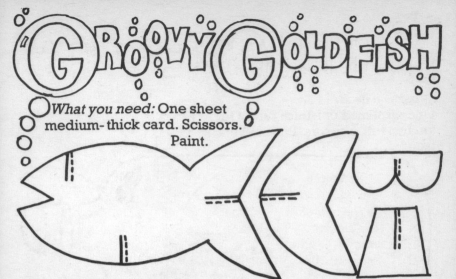

What you need: One sheet medium-thick card. Scissors. Paint.

What you do:
Cut out a simple fish shape in card, plus a tail fin, a base and some sunglasses. Cut slots into the pieces as shown above. Paint the pieces.

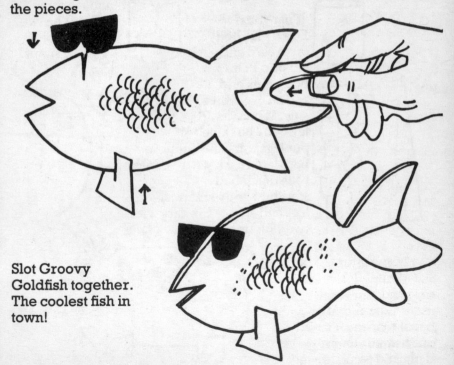

Slot Groovy Goldfish together. The coolest fish in town!

PENELOPE PIG

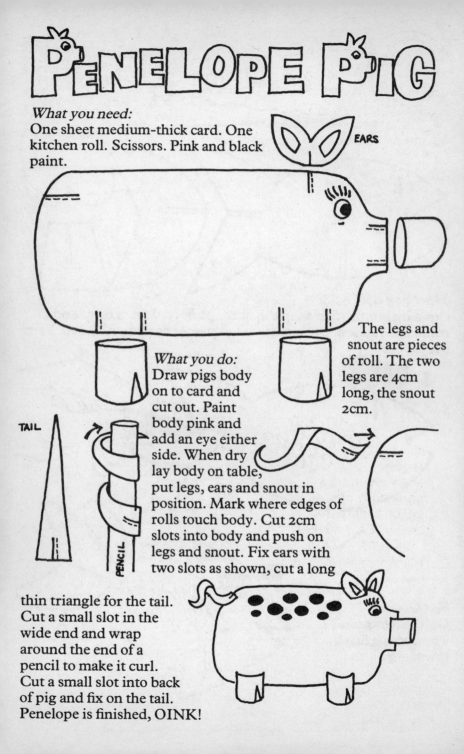

What you need:
One sheet medium-thick card. One kitchen roll. Scissors. Pink and black paint.

EARS

What you do:
Draw pigs body on to card and cut out. Paint body pink and add an eye either side. When dry lay body on table, put legs, ears and snout in position. Mark where edges of rolls touch body. Cut 2cm slots into body and push on legs and snout. Fix ears with two slots as shown, cut a long

The legs and snout are pieces of roll. The two legs are 4cm long, the snout 2cm.

TAIL

PENCIL

thin triangle for the tail. Cut a small slot in the wide end and wrap around the end of a pencil to make it curl. Cut a small slot into back of pig and fix on the tail. Penelope is finished, OINK!

ERNEST the ELEPHANT

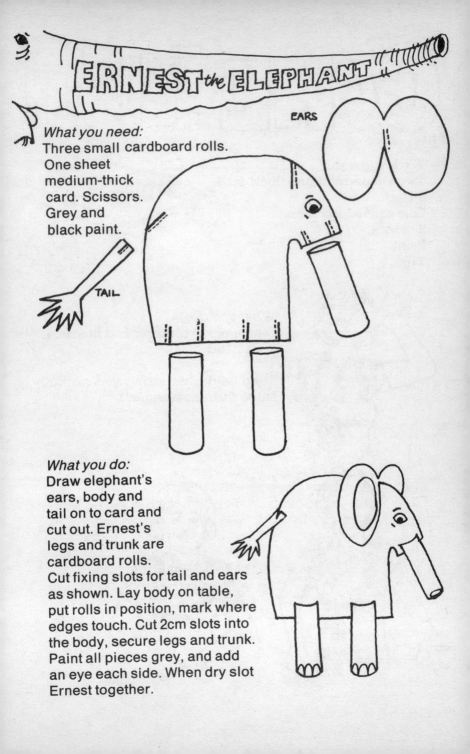

EARS

TAIL

What you need:
Three small cardboard rolls.
One sheet
medium-thick
card. Scissors.
Grey and
black paint.

What you do:
Draw elephant's
ears, body and
tail on to card and
cut out. Ernest's
legs and trunk are
cardboard rolls.
Cut fixing slots for tail and ears
as shown. Lay body on table,
put rolls in position, mark where
edges touch. Cut 2cm slots into
the body, secure legs and trunk.
Paint all pieces grey, and add
an eye each side. When dry slot
Ernest together.

CONE SHAPE HAT

What you need:
Two sheets medium- thick card.
String.
One cardboard roll.
Scissors.
Paint.
Tape.

What you do:
Take a piece of string and measure your head.

Keep hold of the string and carefully halve the measurement.

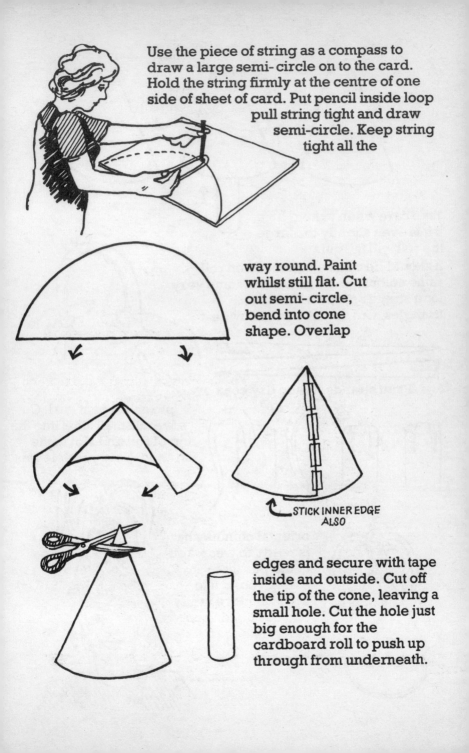

Use the piece of string as a compass to draw a large semi-circle on to the card. Hold the string firmly at the centre of one side of sheet of card. Put pencil inside loop pull string tight and draw semi-circle. Keep string tight all the

way round. Paint whilst still flat. Cut out semi-circle, bend into cone shape. Overlap

STICK INNER EDGE ALSO

edges and secure with tape inside and outside. Cut off the tip of the cone, leaving a small hole. Cut the hole just big enough for the cardboard roll to push up through from underneath.

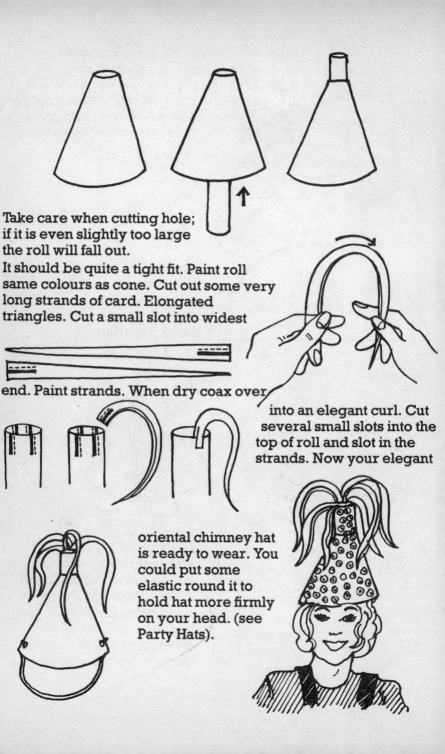

Take care when cutting hole; if it is even slightly too large the roll will fall out.

It should be quite a tight fit. Paint roll same colours as cone. Cut out some very long strands of card. Elongated triangles. Cut a small slot into widest

end. Paint strands. When dry coax over into an elegant curl. Cut several small slots into the top of roll and slot in the strands. Now your elegant

oriental chimney hat is ready to wear. You could put some elastic round it to hold hat more firmly on your head. (see Party Hats).

PARTY HATS

What you need:
Medium-thick card. Scissors. Paint. Tape. A dinner plate. Thin elastic.

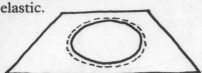

What you do:
Lay the plate face down on to a sheet of card. Draw round it and cut the circle out.

Fold circle in half and cut along the crease giving you two semi-circles. Each semi-circle will make one hat. Decorate whilst hats are still flat. Paint name of guest along the curved side of the semi-circle. When paint is dry take a

corner in each hand and gently bend round into a cone shape. Overlap the edges and secure with tape inside and outside.

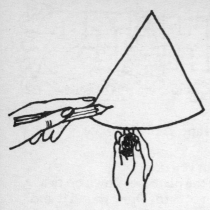

Make a small hole either side of hat. Do this with a sharp pencil and a small lump of plasticine. Hold the plasticine inside the hat against the card where you want the hole.

Push pencil through card into the plasticine. This way you cannot slip and stab yourself.

Measure a length of elastic to fit round your head, and under your chin. Thread elastic through holes and secure with a knot each side. You could vary the cones by giving some of them petal tops instead of points.

Cut off the very tips of the hat. Make downward cuts (2 to 3cms) round the top.

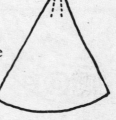

Fold out the petals. Trim them into points or curves. Paint the insides of the petals for extra effect.

The hats can also be varied by adding shapes cut out of card.

Long 'fronds' are quite effective. Cut out long strips of card, one end tapering into points. Coax pointed end over so that the frond gently curves. Stick the wider end with tape on to the back of hat.

Put one or two on each hat. Feather shapes are also easy to cut out. Now you have lots of different hats. Your guests will be thrilled to have hats with their names on!

PARTY TIME

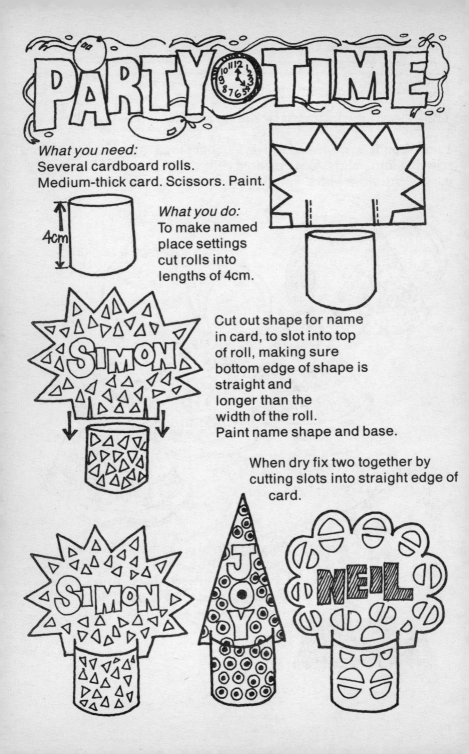

What you need:
Several cardboard rolls.
Medium-thick card. Scissors. Paint.

What you do:
To make named place settings cut rolls into lengths of 4cm.

4cm

Cut out shape for name in card, to slot into top of roll, making sure bottom edge of shape is straight and longer than the width of the roll.
Paint name shape and base.

When dry fix two together by cutting slots into straight edge of card.

SIMON

JOY

NEIL

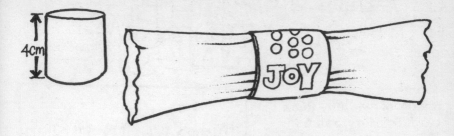

Cut rolls into 4cm lengths and paint on names to make serviette holders.

Now each of your guests has their own hat, place setting for the table, and serviette ring.

STAND UP BIRTHDAY CARDS

What you need:
Sheets of medium-thick card. Scissors. Paint.

What you do:
Cut out two rectangles of card the same size. Cut a slot halfway up the centre of one piece and halfway down the centre of the other. Write 'Happy' to the left of each slot and 'Birthday' to the right. Turn both pieces over and repeat on the other side. Slot the two pieces together, and the card will read 'Happy Birthday' all the way round.

Cut out a smaller rectangle with a slot centre bottom. Paint birthday name on both sides of card. Slot it on to top of birthday card. You now have a personalised stand up birthday card.

Once you have the basic idea you can vary the card.
What about a parcel with a ribbon on top?

You could even change the shape

from a rectangle, as long as you keep the basic slot cuts. Here is a zig-zag card made the same way with a 'Many Happy Returns'

message. 'Happy Returns' is written either side of main piece and 'Many' on to a smaller piece fixed on top.

BIRTHDAY CAKE

What you need:
One cardboard box (about size of cake).
One sheet medium-thick card.
Scissors. Craft knife. Paint.

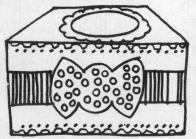

What you do:
Fold flaps of cardboard box in to make cube. Paint to look like a cake. Use sugary colours and paint a bright ribbon all round with a big bow at the front.

Cut small and very thin slots into the top of the cake where you want to place the candles. (I put mine in a circle.)

Cut candles out of sheet of card, leave a good base at the end of each candle to push into slots on cake.

YELLOW
RED
BLUE

4cm.

Paint candles different colours. Remember to paint both sides. The candle flame is made up of yellow, red and blue.

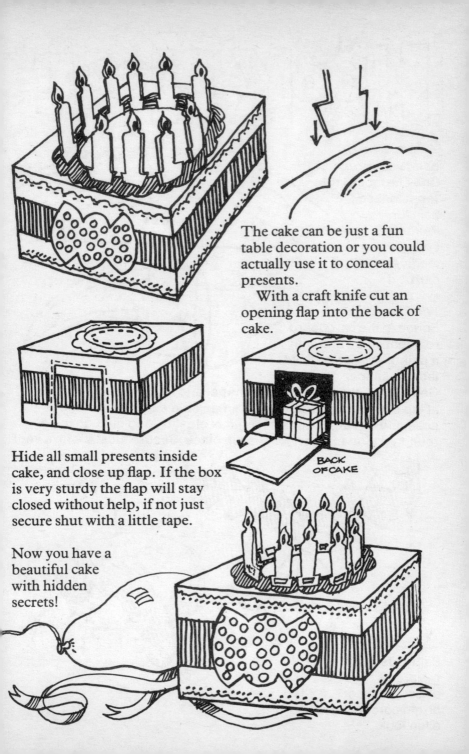

The cake can be just a fun table decoration or you could actually use it to conceal presents.

With a craft knife cut an opening flap into the back of cake.

BACK OF CAKE

Hide all small presents inside cake, and close up flap. If the box is very sturdy the flap will stay closed without help, if not just secure shut with a little tape.

Now you have a beautiful cake with hidden secrets!

HOOK NOSE

What you need:
One cardboard roll.
Tape. Elastic.
Scissors.
Paint.
Scrap of
medium-thick
card.

What you do:
Squeeze the cardboard
roll gently flat, and with
a pair of scissors cut out
the two shapes as shown.
Gently coax the roll back into shape, and tape the two edges
at top of nose together. Make a small hole either side of the
nose and thread through a length of elastic, long enough to go
round your head and hold nose in place. Secure elastic with a knot
at each end. Cut out some
heavy eyebrows to fix
into a slot
cut into bridge of nose
for extra effect.

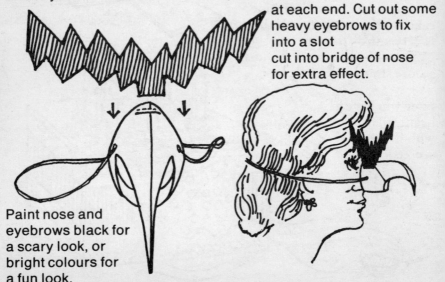

Paint nose and
eyebrows black for
a scary look, or
bright colours for
a fun look.

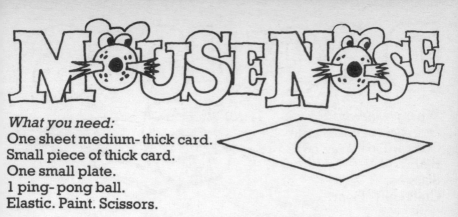

MOUSE NOSE

What you need:
One sheet medium-thick card.
Small piece of thick card.
One small plate.
1 ping-pong ball.
Elastic. Paint. Scissors.

What you do: Draw round plate on to card and cut out circle. Cut a section from the circle a little less than a semi-circle. Roll this section into a thin cone and secure with tape overlapping edges slightly.

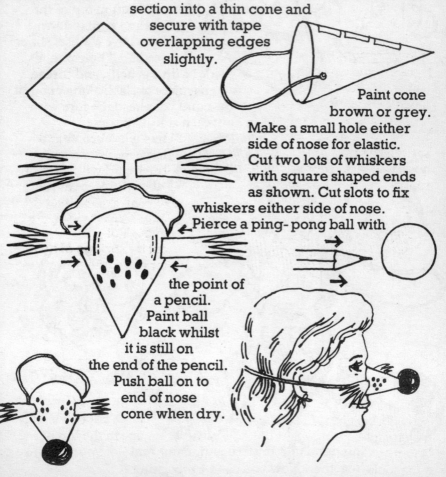

Paint cone brown or grey. Make a small hole either side of nose for elastic. Cut two lots of whiskers with square shaped ends as shown. Cut slots to fix whiskers either side of nose. Pierce a ping-pong ball with the point of a pencil. Paint ball black whilst it is still on the end of the pencil. Push ball on to end of nose cone when dry.

DISGUISES

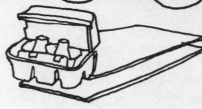

What you need:
One sheet of thick card.
One cardboard egg box.
Elastic.
Scissors.
Craft knife. Paint.

What you do:
Cut one section out of the
egg box and trim it down
until you have a 'nose' shape.
Pierce a small hole either
side (with a pencil), and thread
through a piece of elastic long enough
to go round your head. Secure with
a knot each side. Cut some
bushy eyebrows and a
large moustache out of
thick card with a square
'slotting' piece at the
centre of each.

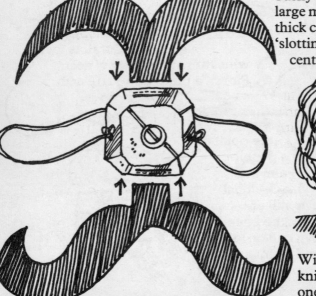

With the craft
knife cut two slots,
one in the top of the
nose and one underneath. Paint and slot your disguise
together. Now you can be incognito.

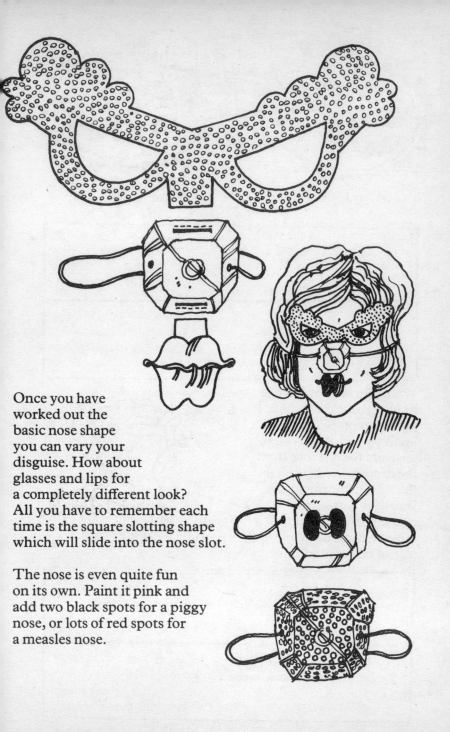

Once you have
worked out the
basic nose shape
you can vary your
disguise. How about
glasses and lips for
a completely different look?
All you have to remember each
time is the square slotting shape
which will slide into the nose slot.

The nose is even quite fun
on its own. Paint it pink and
add two black spots for a piggy
nose, or lots of red spots for
a measles nose.

SPECTACLES

What you need: One large sheet medium-thick card. A ruler. Scissors. Paint.

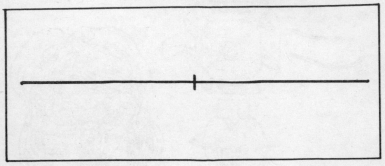

What you do: Draw a line right across card and mark a centre point. Hold the ruler up to your face and roughly measure the distance from the centre of your nose to the side of your head. (Be generous with all the measurements.) Put this measurement down either side of centre mark.

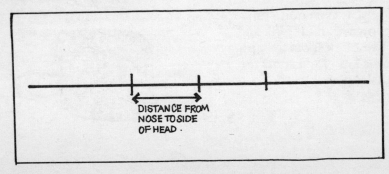

DISTANCE FROM NOSE TO SIDE OF HEAD.

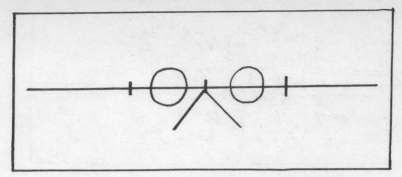

Draw circle in each space big enough to be the 'eyeholes'. Starting from centre point, draw two sides of a triangle, an upside-down V. This is where you will cut a space for your nose. Hold up the ruler again and measure from the side of your head to the top of your ear. Put this measurement down either side.

Draw in the 'arms' of the glasses starting at A, and curving them round at B. Now you can make the glasses any shape you like.

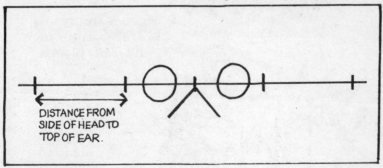

DISTANCE FROM SIDE OF HEAD TO TOP OF EAR.

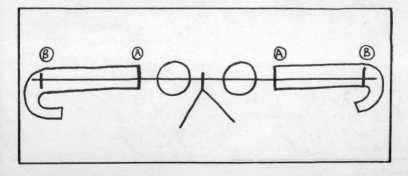

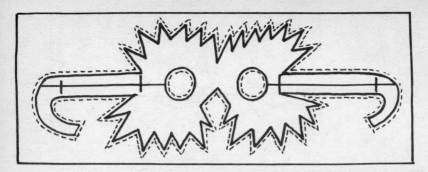

Once you have finished drawing the glasses, carefully cut them out. Take care when cutting out the eyeholes. Start cut by piercing card with a pencil. You could even zig-zag the eyeholes as I have done below. Paint the glasses.

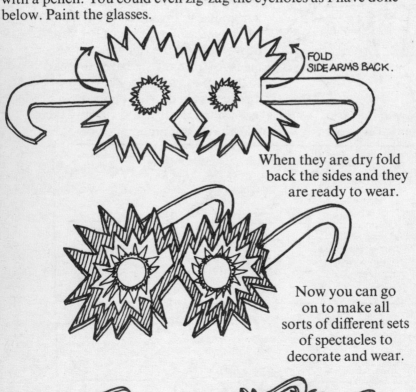

FOLD SIDE ARMS BACK.

When they are dry fold back the sides and they are ready to wear.

Now you can go on to make all sorts of different sets of spectacles to decorate and wear.

Traffic Lights

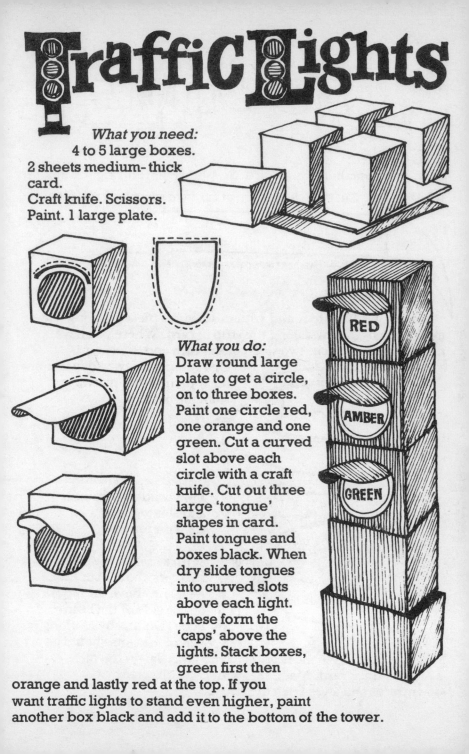

What you need:
4 to 5 large boxes.
2 sheets medium- thick card.
Craft knife. Scissors.
Paint. 1 large plate.

What you do:
Draw round large plate to get a circle, on to three boxes. Paint one circle red, one orange and one green. Cut a curved slot above each circle with a craft knife. Cut out three large 'tongue' shapes in card. Paint tongues and boxes black. When dry slide tongues into curved slots above each light. These form the 'caps' above the lights. Stack boxes, green first then orange and lastly red at the top. If you want traffic lights to stand even higher, paint another box black and add it to the bottom of the tower.

BIG CHIEF

What you need:
2 to 3 sheets medium-thick card. Scissors. Paint. String. Craft knife.

What you do: Cut out a long strip of card with curved ends about

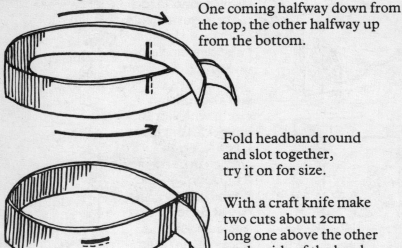

MEASUREMENT TO FIT ROUND HEAD

70cms long. Measure round your head with a piece of string and mark the length down along the strip of card. Where you have marked the length cut two slots, one at each end.

One coming halfway down from the top, the other halfway up from the bottom.

Fold headband round and slot together, try it on for size.

With a craft knife make two cuts about 2cm long one above the other on the side of the head-band. Do this by marking where the slots should go with a pencil. Undo the headband and lay it flat on top of a piece of thick card. Make cuts with knife directed downwards and away from the body.

PAINTED FEATHER

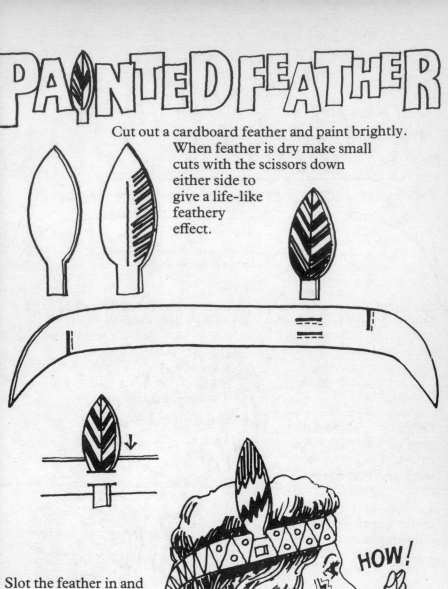

Cut out a cardboard feather and paint brightly. When feather is dry make small cuts with the scissors down either side to give a life-like feathery effect.

Slot the feather in and out of the two cuts on the headband. Fix the headband together and put it on. You could give yourself a Red-Indian face using face paints.

HOW!

Make a Chief's head-dress the same way. Cut out lots of feathers and arrange them along the headband. Have large feathers at the centre

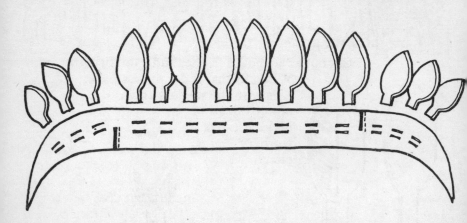

and smaller ones at the sides. Make two cuts for each feather to fix into. Keep the feathers about 2cm from either side of the

fixing slots. If the cuts get too close to the slots the band will become weak and may break.

Look at real feathers to get lots of painting ideas.

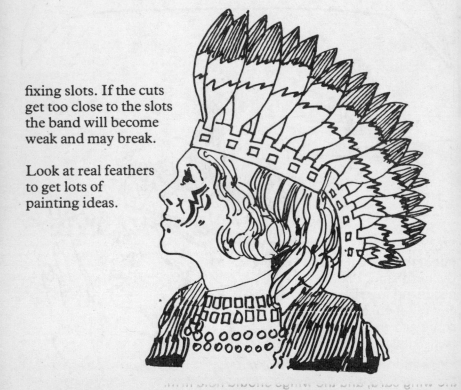

TOTEM POLE

What you need:
Lots of large cardboard boxes (it doesn't matter if they are different shapes.)
Paint.
Craft knife. Scissors.
What you do:
The Totem Pole is made by stacking the boxes one on top of another to form a tower. Paint the boxes with bright colours with lots of zig-zag shapes, animal and bird faces to give Totem a Red-Indian feel. You could have a large bird at the top of the Totem Pole.

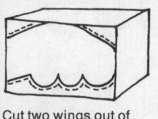
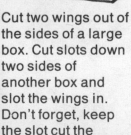

Cut two wings out of the sides of a large box. Cut slots down two sides of another box and slot the wings in. Don't forget, keep the slot cut the same thickness as the wing card, and the wings should hold firm.

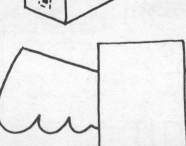

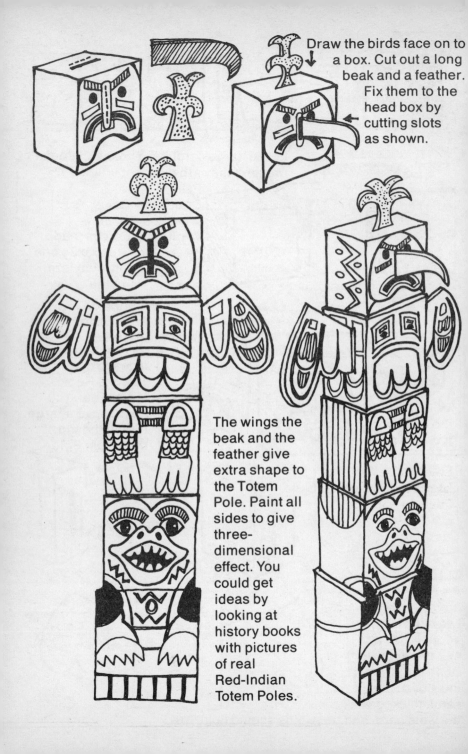

Draw the birds face on to a box. Cut out a long beak and a feather. Fix them to the head box by cutting slots as shown.

The wings the beak and the feather give extra shape to the Totem Pole. Paint all sides to give three-dimensional effect. You could get ideas by looking at history books with pictures of real Red-Indian Totem Poles.

THE PAPER CUP GAME

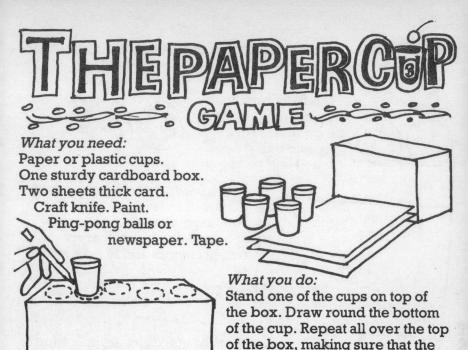

What you need:
Paper or plastic cups.
One sturdy cardboard box.
Two sheets thick card.
Craft knife. Paint.
Ping-pong balls or
newspaper. Tape.

What you do:
Stand one of the cups on top of the box. Draw round the bottom of the cup. Repeat all over the top of the box, making sure that the circles do not overlap, and that there is about a 2cm gap between each circle.

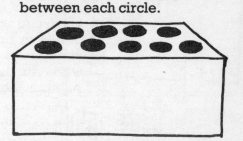

With a craft knife cut all the circles out. As you have drawn round the bottom of the cup, the hole wll be slightly bigger than the cup base. Push the cups into the holes and they should stand firm.

Take the cups out and paint the box and the cups bright colours. There are some types of plastic cups that will not easily take paint. Thick water base paint and a large brush are probably best.

Stick on a piece of circular card, or paint straight on to each cup, a number between one and four.

The balls can either be ping-pong balls or newspapers screwed up into ball shapes taped and painted.

As a backdrop for the game take a large sheet of thick card. Cut two 'base' shapes, cut slots as shown. Paint the back drop bright colours and stand it up.

Stand the box with the cups in, in front of the backdrop on the floor or on a table. Take it in turns to throw five balls each. Every time you get a ball into a cup you score the number of points on the cup. Keep score, after ten goes each, whoever has the most points is the winner.

COCONUT SHY.

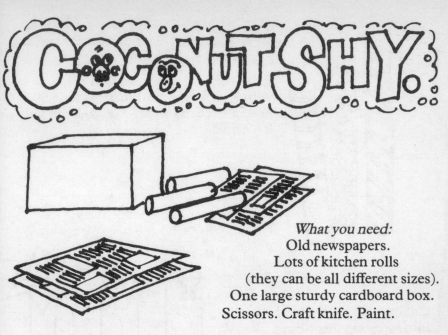

What you need:
Old newspapers.
Lots of kitchen rolls
(they can be all different sizes).
One large sturdy cardboard box.
Scissors. Craft knife. Paint.

What you do:

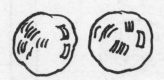

Scrunch newspaper into round ball shapes, slightly larger than tennis balls. Use tape to fix balls together keeping the tape to one side forming a 'seam'. These balls are the coconuts.

Paint coconuts brown. You could paint a different face on to each coconut.

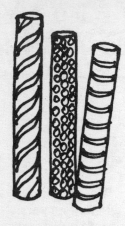

Paint the kitchen rolls bright colours with lots of spots and stripes. You will need a kitchen roll for each coconut you have made.

Cut one end of each kitchen roll into a zig-zag shape by cutting V shapes out of card with scissors about 4cm deep all round. Splay the points out creating a petal shape providing a base for the coconut to sit on.

Hold the bottom end of each kitchen roll so that it stands on top surface of the box. Draw round each roll and cut out circular holes with a craft knife, keeping the cut just inside the drawn line. If the holes are the right size the rolls should wedge firmly into them standing upright. Take out the rolls and paint the box brightly.

Make the balls to throw, the same way as you made the coconuts, only smaller, about the size of ping-pong balls.

Push the kitchen rolls into their holes. Balance the coconuts on top. Stand back with the balls and you are ready for a game!

BOX THEATRE

What you need:
One sturdy cardboard box with flaps folded in to form a cube. Sheets of medium-thick card. Craft knife. Ruler. Scissors. Paint.

What you do: With a craft knife, cut a rectangle out of the front of the box leaving a good border all round.

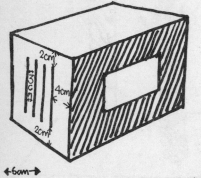

With a ruler and a pencil mark series of lines down each side of the box. Keep the lines about 3cm apart. Leave 2cms top and bottom and start the first line 4cm in from the front. With the craft knife cut the lines into slots. These slots are where the scenes slide through. Cut the scenes out of medium-thick card.

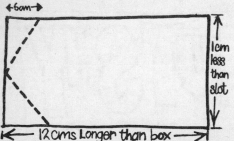

Width: 1cm less than the length of slot.
Length: 12cm longer than box. Mark 6cm in from one

end and cut into a point. Hold the card and push the point through the front slot on the right side of the box. Guide the card through and out of the left hand slot by holding it from underneath the box. From the front you can see how much of the card will be showing. Mark this area with a pencil and take the scene out. Make the cards to fit all the slots and paint scenes on each one. You could use a fairy story or make up your own.

You need one more slot along the top of the box 2cms back from the front. Leave 2cms either end of slot as before.

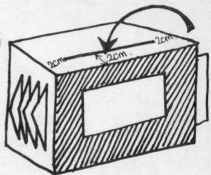

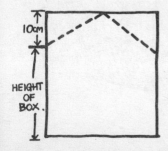

This slot is for the curtain. Cut the curtain out of a piece of card. It should be about 10cm taller than the height of the box and wide enough to fit the slot. Trim top into a point.

Paint the top triangle black and design a red curtain below.

Paint the front of the box and all the bits of card sticking out at the sides black, to give an overall dark and theatrical effect.

Design your own theatre emblem to go across the top of the box. Slide in the scenes in the right order. Lower the curtain and you are ready for a show. You could turn off the light and shine a torch at the theatre for extra atmosphere!

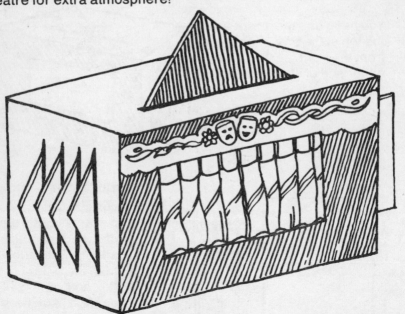

AEROPLANE

What you need:
One sheet thick card.
Scissors.
Craft knife.
Paint.

What you do:
Cut the body of the plane out of the card.
Cut three slots as shown. (For the slots
along the body, you will need
the craft knife.) Cut out tail plane (1) to
fit slot and a circle with a small slot in
the centre (2). This is the propeller,
whizzing round.

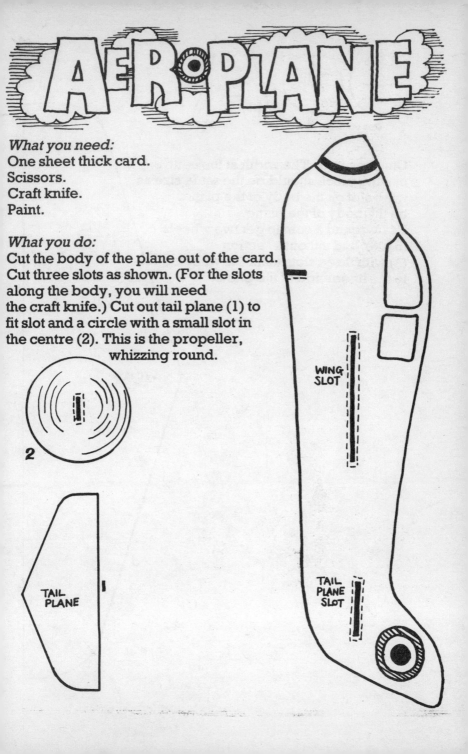

2

TAIL
PLANE

WING
SLOT

TAIL
PLANE
SLOT

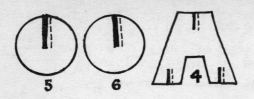

Cut out wings. The width at the centre
of wing piece should be the same size as
wing slot on the body of the plane.
on the body of the plane.
Draw round a coin to get two wheels
(5 & 6), and cut out a section
(4) with three slots to fix the wheels
to the underside of the plane.

WINGS

3

Paint all the separate pieces (leave propeller circle white and just add some black movement lines.) When dry slot plane together. The plane will stand up on its own, or you could have it in flight, by hanging it from a thread attached to the top of the body.

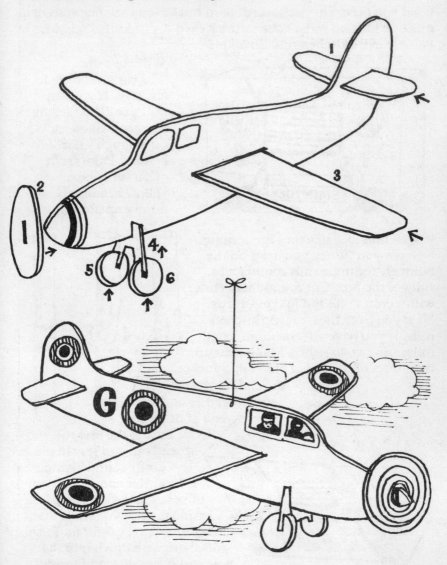

CAR SCULPTURE

What you need: One large cardboard box. 2 long kitchen rolls or 4 medium kitchen rolls. 2 sheets thick card. Craft knife. Scissors. Paint. 1 extra kitchen roll. Small plate.

What you do:
The car can be made any size. If you can find a really large box you can make a car big enough to sit behind. Paint front of car on to box: yellow headlights, a number plate and wheels that look like they are coming towards you. When you draw on the bumper, continue ends round on to sides of the box. Cut round these ends with a craft knife and fold outwards. Next you need the two long kitchen rolls. If you have only medium length rolls, join two together. Make a cut up both sides of the end of one roll. Squeeze the ends of the roll gently together and slide into end of other roll.

Once inside, the first roll will spread out and stay in place. Draw round kitchen rolls either end of top surface of box. Cut holes. Keep holes inside the drawn line so that the roll is a very tight fit. Push roll about 4cm down into the hole and it should stand firmly in place.

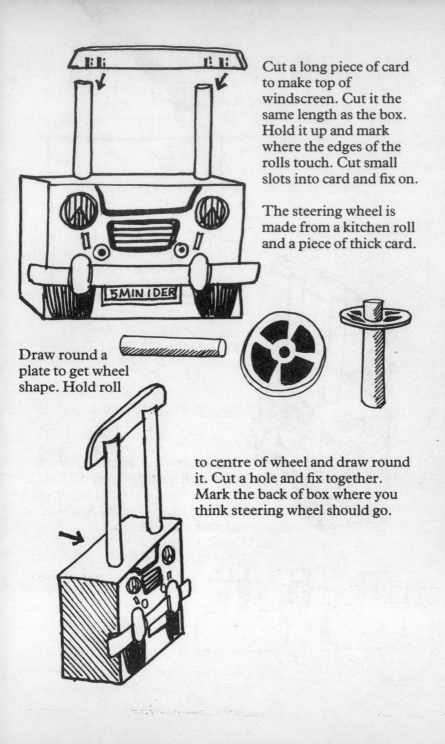

Cut a long piece of card
to make top of
windscreen. Cut it the
same length as the box.
Hold it up and mark
where the edges of the
rolls touch. Cut small
slots into card and fix on.

The steering wheel is
made from a kitchen roll
and a piece of thick card.

Draw round a
plate to get wheel
shape. Hold roll

to centre of wheel and draw round
it. Cut a hole and fix together.
Mark the back of box where you
think steering wheel should go.

5 MIN 1 DER

Draw round the other end of the roll, and cut hole just inside drawn line.

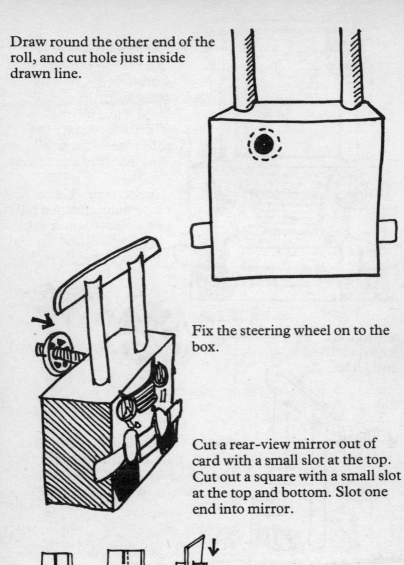

Fix the steering wheel on to the box.

Cut a rear-view mirror out of card with a small slot at the top. Cut out a square with a small slot at the top and bottom. Slot one end into mirror.

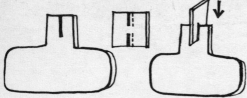

Slot the other end into a slot cut up halfway along the top of windscreen. Design and cut out a little emblem to fix into top of bonnet.

Cut a small slot for it to fix into.
Choose a bright colour and paint car. If it is large enough, you can sit behind the box and drive.

If you only have a small box, make a tiny car and stand it up on a shelf.

SLIPPERY SNAKE

What you need: One sheet medium-thick card.
Scissors. Paint.

What you do: Draw three snake sections along the straight edge of a piece of card (head, middle, tail), giving each section a flat base which will help the snake to stand up. Overlap each section by about 3cm as shown. Cut 1.5cm slots to join sections together. Cut out a forked tongue and a rattle, each with slot cuts. Cut small slots into Slippery's mouth and at the very tip of his tail and fix on the tongue and rattle.

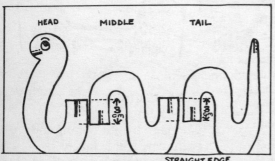

HEAD   MIDDLE   TAIL

STRAIGHT EDGE.

Paint both sides of snakes body and slot together when dry. If you want to make him longer, add more middle sections. Slippery can be as long as you like.

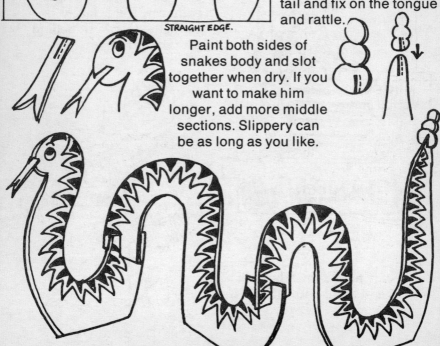

CRUNCHER CROCODILE

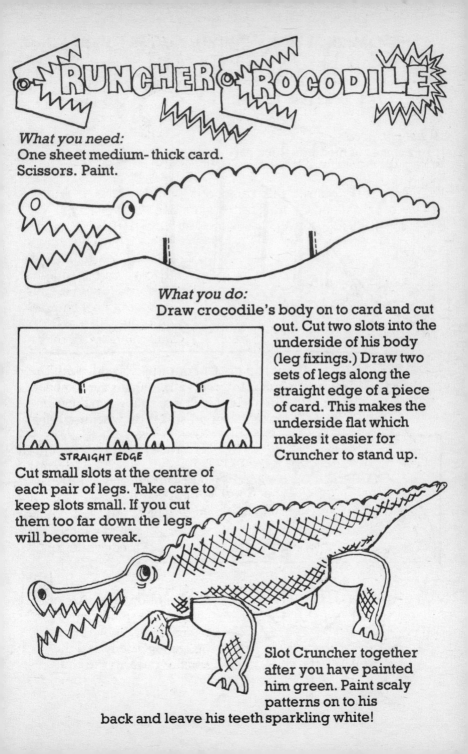

What you need:
One sheet medium-thick card.
Scissors. Paint.

What you do:
Draw crocodile's body on to card and cut out. Cut two slots into the underside of his body (leg fixings.) Draw two sets of legs along the straight edge of a piece of card. This makes the underside flat which makes it easier for Cruncher to stand up.

STRAIGHT EDGE

Cut small slots at the centre of each pair of legs. Take care to keep slots small. If you cut them too far down the legs will become weak.

Slot Cruncher together after you have painted him green. Paint scaly patterns on to his back and leave his teeth sparkling white!

SPIKY HEDGEHOG

What you need:
1 to 2 sheets of medium-thick card.
Scissors.
Paint.

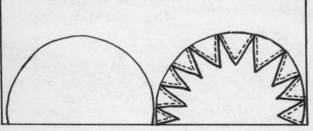

What you do: Cut out Spiky's body with slots at regular intervals all along his curved back. The first set of spikes are shown in diagram 1. To make the larger spikes draw semi-circles

(they do not need to be accurate) along the edge of card. Cut out semi-circles and cut the curved edge into spikes.

Cut a slot up the centre of shape. The spike shapes get bigger as you move along the hedgehog's body and then get smaller towards the end.

Match up the slot in each piece of card to the slot in the body. The shapes should push down so that the straight edge at the bottom meets the straight edge of the body, and will stand flat on the table. The spike shapes at the back will need to be smaller as they fix into the body at an angle. Colour Spiky black and brown, or you could paint each spike a different colour for a rainbow hedgehog!

Septimus
SPIDER

What you need: One sheet medium-thick card. Scissors. Compass. Paint.

What you do: Draw two circles the same size with a compass and pencil on to the card. Carefully follow the instructions drawn below.

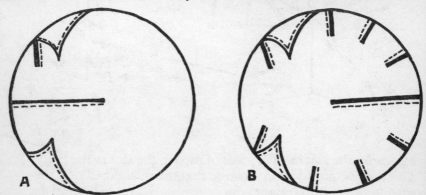

Each circle has a small section cut out of each side leaving a head and body. They should look like the outlines of fat number eights lying on their side. A has a slot from the front of head to centre of circle, and a small slot in head section. B has a slot from centre of circle to back of body, and eight small slots at regular intervals round the body. Next you need to make the legs. Draw one leg (as below) and cut it out. Draw round the first leg seven times, so that all legs are the same.

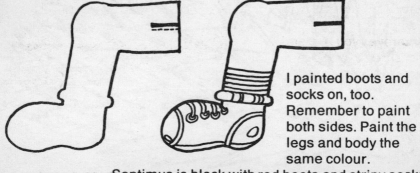

I painted boots and socks on, too. Remember to paint both sides. Paint the legs and body the same colour.

Septimus is black with red boots and stripy socks.

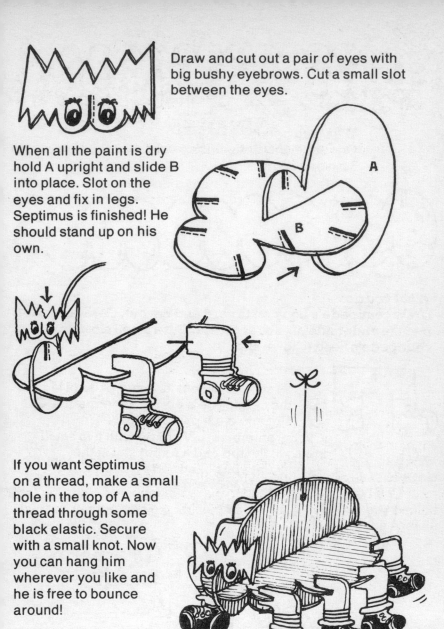

Draw and cut out a pair of eyes with big bushy eyebrows. Cut a small slot between the eyes.

When all the paint is dry hold A upright and slide B into place. Slot on the eyes and fix in legs. Septimus is finished! He should stand up on his own.

If you want Septimus on a thread, make a small hole in the top of A and thread through some black elastic. Secure with a small knot. Now you can hang him wherever you like and he is free to bounce around!

CLIVE · CENTIPEDE

What you need:
One sheet medium-thick card.
Scissors. Paint.

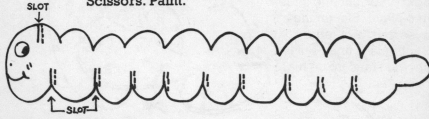

SLOT

SLOT

What you do:
Draw centipede's body on to card and cut out. Cut a small slot into the underside of each segment. Cut a small slot into centipede's head (shown above).

Draw and cut out as many pairs of legs as the centipede's body has segments. Cut slot into each pair of legs.
Cut out antennae, a V shape with two small circles at the top and a fixing slot at the bottom. Paint your centipede a bright colour (mine was orange).
Slot centipede together.
If you like the result you could go on to make an even longer one!

VENTRILOQUIST'S DUMMY

What you need:
Two sheets medium-thick card.
Tape. Paint. Scissors.

What you do:
Draw head and shoulders
of dummy on to sheet of
card. Draw only the top lip
of the mouth. Mark out a
shape underneath top lip as
shown above.

Carefully cut out this shape. Start the
cut by piercing the card with a pencil to
get a small hole to insert the scissors.

Cut a strip off the side of the second
sheet of card so that it is narrower
than the first. Lay the second
sheet under the first leaving 6cm
showing at the bottom.

6cm

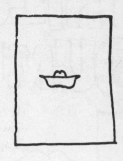

Draw lower lip on to second sheet of card whilst in position (1). Pull out to colour (2).

Colour the space above lower lip black. You could include a small tongue as I have done. Colour the lower part of the card the same shade as dummy's skin. Colour top and bottom lip bright red for maximum effect.

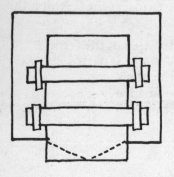

When dry place second sheet of card in place and carefully turn two sheets over, taking care not to move them out of position. Secure second sheet by laying two longer strips of card right across the back and taping them down. Cut the bit of card sticking out at the bottom into a point.

The pointed end makes the second
sheet of card easier to move up and
down.

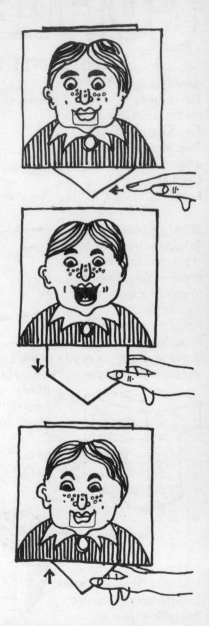

Hold the head card steady
with one hand and gently pull
second card downwards. The
dummy opens his mouth.

Push the card back up
and the dummy shuts
his mouth. Move the dummy's
mouth as you speak and he will
appear to do the talking!

'GOTTLER GEER'

THE VENTRILOQUIST'S DUMMY

What you need:
Two sturdy cardboard boxes, one
larger than the other.
Two kitchen rolls.
Two sheets of thick card or
an extra box to cut up.
Craft knife.
Paint. Tape.

What you do:
Take smaller box and
cut it into two as
shown. You may need
to reinforce the seams
with tape after cutting.
Paint dummy's face
on to front of box. The

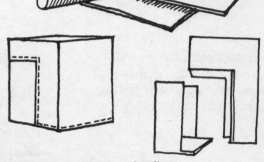

moving mouth is made in the same way as the flat
version of the dummy (see page 63). Paint on
only upper lip and cut a rectangular hole
beneath. Leave about 4cm underneath the
face (this is to fix head to body).
Cut a slot along top surface of head to
secure hair. The hair is cut from thick card
4cm with a square shape in the centre to fix

into slot. You will need
to carefully measure
the hair-piece and
trim it, so that it fits
snugly over the box.

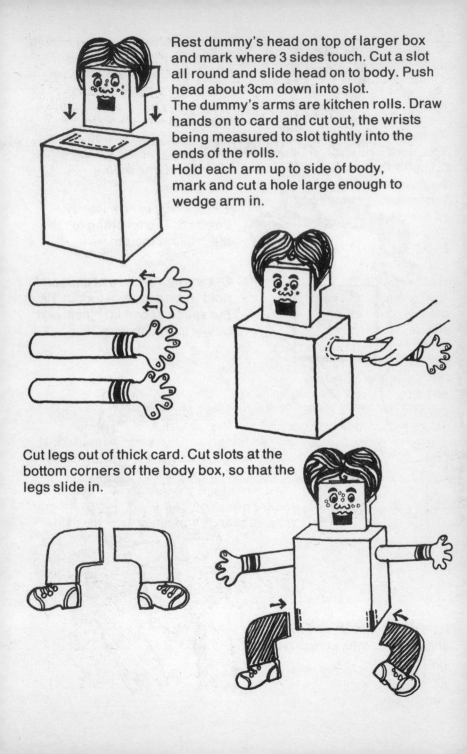

Rest dummy's head on top of larger box and mark where 3 sides touch. Cut a slot all round and slide head on to body. Push head about 3cm down into slot.

The dummy's arms are kitchen rolls. Draw hands on to card and cut out, the wrists being measured to slot tightly into the ends of the rolls.

Hold each arm up to side of body, mark and cut a hole large enough to wedge arm in.

Cut legs out of thick card. Cut slots at the bottom corners of the body box, so that the legs slide in.

Paint a black strip round bottom part of body box. Paint legs black (with different coloured boots). When you slot legs in, the dummy will appear to have black trousers on. Paint upper half of body to look like a jacket, giving arms the same colour.

The dummy is now nearly finished. The finishing touch is the moving mouth.

Cut a small square of card and hold it up to back of mouth. Paint the space above lip black, and below to match face.

Hold card in place and move up and down to make the dummy speak.

MONTY MONKEY

What you need:
4 to 5 large cardboard boxes.
Four long kitchen rolls.
Thick card.
Craft knife.
Paint.

What you do:
Before you start, stack the boxes up to decide on the overall shape of the monkey. Choose the smallest squarest box for the head. Paint top part of monkey's face on to box.

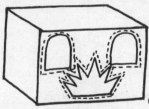

Cut out two cardboard ears and a tuft of hair, from either a sheet of card or from

the side of another box. Cut three slots into the head box, at the top for the hair, and at the sides for the ears.

Paint the lower part of monkey's face on to the next box. Draw on the top part of his chest.

Take a kitchen roll and mark the arm holes on this box. Draw round the end of the roll and cut the hole just inside drawn line, so the roll fits tightly into the hole.

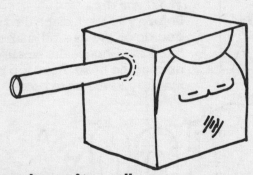

Each arm is made up of two rolls.
Hold the end of one roll up to the second roll. Mark and cut out circle as shown below. The first roll should fit snugly into the second one forming an elbow. This join needs to be secure. You may need to add a little tape if the hole is cut even slightly too large.

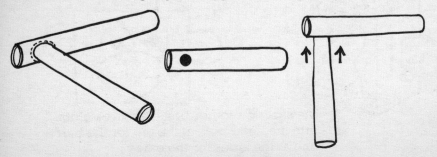

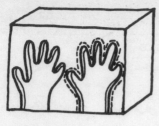

Draw the hands on to thick card.
Cut them out. Secure them to arms
with slots. Hold the roll up to the
hand and mark where
the edge of the roll
touches. Cut slots into
the hand and a slot
either side of each roll.
Fix the hand on to the
end of arm.

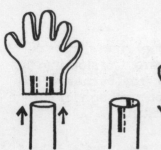

Draw the monkey's stomach and tummy
button on to the next box.

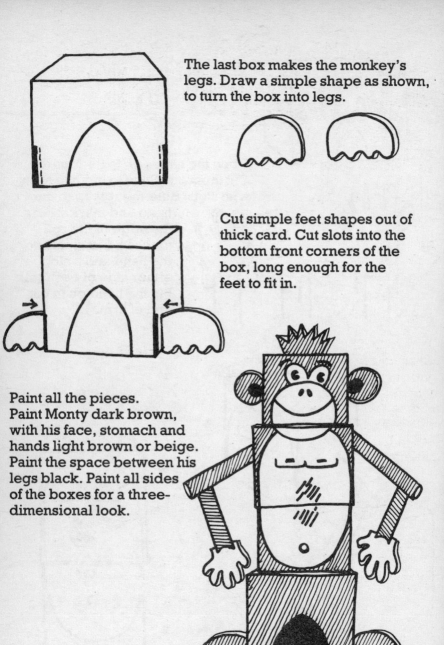

The last box makes the monkey's legs. Draw a simple shape as shown, to turn the box into legs.

Cut simple feet shapes out of thick card. Cut slots into the bottom front corners of the box, long enough for the feet to fit in.

Paint all the pieces. Paint Monty dark brown, with his face, stomach and hands light brown or beige. Paint the space between his legs black. Paint all sides of the boxes for a three-dimensional look.

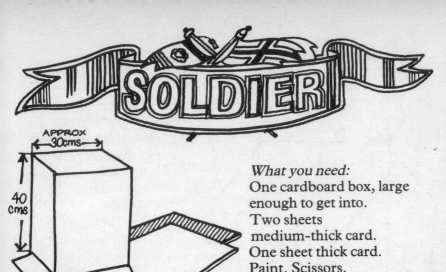

SOLDIER

APPROX 30cms

40 cms

What you need:
One cardboard box, large enough to get into.
Two sheets medium-thick card.
One sheet thick card.
Paint. Scissors.
Craft knife. Tape.

What you do:
Cut a hole at the top of the box with a craft knife, large enough for your head to fit through. Cut holes for your arms either side of the box so that you can pull it over your head like a jumper and wear it.

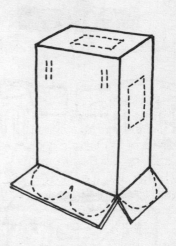

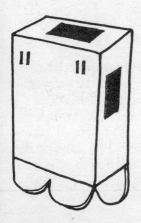

Leave the flaps on the bottom of the box, but round off the corners so that they look like the flaps on a jacket.

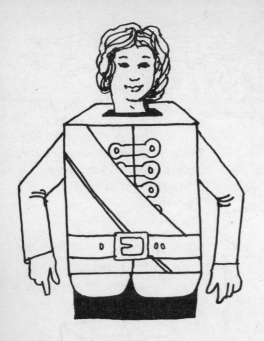

Paint the box bright red. Paint on a belt, sash and buttons, using bright yellow and black.

Cut out two epaulettes in thick card. Leave a square flap on the insides, to fix them to the uniform.

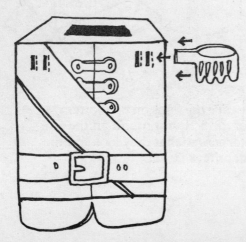

Cut two slots either side on the front of the box about shoulder height. The two slots should be about 3cms apart. The flaps on the epaulettes should be trimmed to fit snugly into these slots.

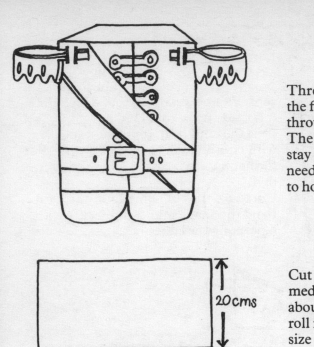

Thread epaulette into the first slot and out through the second. The epaulettes should stay in place, you may need a little tape just to hold them firm.

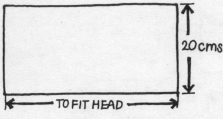

20 cms

TO FIT HEAD

Cut out a piece of medium-thick card about 20cm high to roll into a hat. Test the size over your head.

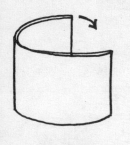

Paint card black and when it is dry roll into a cylinder. Slightly overlap the ends and secure with tape inside and out.

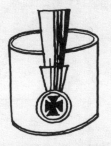

Cut out a cardboard badge or feather and stick it into the front of the hat.

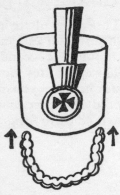

Cut a chin strap out of medium-thick card. Paint it yellow so that it looks like it is made up of chain links.

Curl the chin strap round and stick it with tape on to the inside of the hat. Put the hat on and measure length of strap first.

Cut two cuffs out of medium-thick card. Bend the shape round and secure with tape along the edges.

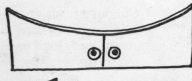

Wear a red jumper or T-shirt underneath the box. Dark trousers and wellington boots would complete the outfit. You could even award yourself a cardboard medal to stick on to your uniform.

SWEETEMAN

What you need:

Four different sized boxes (head, body, waist and legs).
1 triangular chocolate box. 2 kitchen rolls. 2 sheets
thick card.

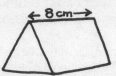

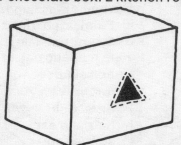

2 sheets
medium-thick card.
Paint Scissors.
Craft knife.

What you do:

Cut a length of
triangular chocolate
box about 8cm. Hold
it up to the centre of the box
that is to be the head and
draw round it. Cut a hole just
inside drawn line with a craft
knife, so triangular nose can
slot in. Cut a small slot into

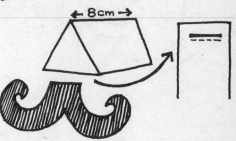

the underside of the nose and cut
out a moustache in medium-thick
card to push up into the slot. Cut
out eyelash shapes (shown
below), in medium-thick card.
Make cuts into them with
scissors leaving 4cm at

BASE   4cm.   BASE

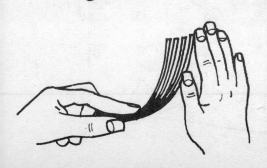

base. Cut two curved
eyelash slots into face.
Gently push fringed end of
eyelash upwards and slot
base into curved slots on
face.

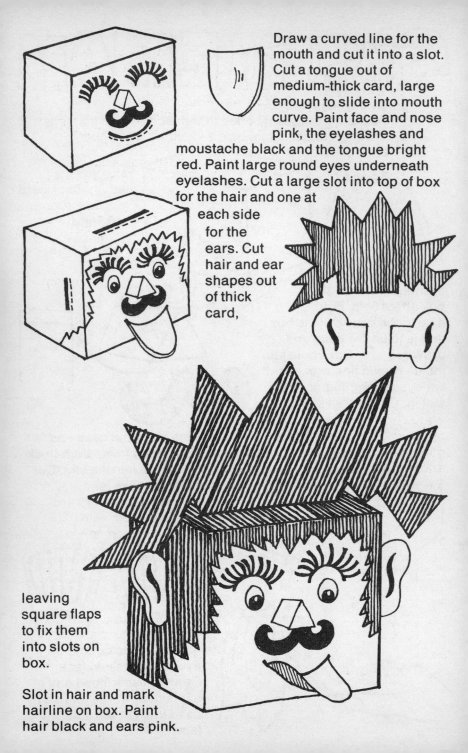

Draw a curved line for the mouth and cut it into a slot. Cut a tongue out of medium-thick card, large enough to slide into mouth curve. Paint face and nose pink, the eyelashes and moustache black and the tongue bright red. Paint large round eyes underneath eyelashes. Cut a large slot into top of box for the hair and one at each side for the ears. Cut hair and ear shapes out of thick card,

leaving square flaps to fix them into slots on box.

Slot in hair and mark hairline on box. Paint hair black and ears pink.

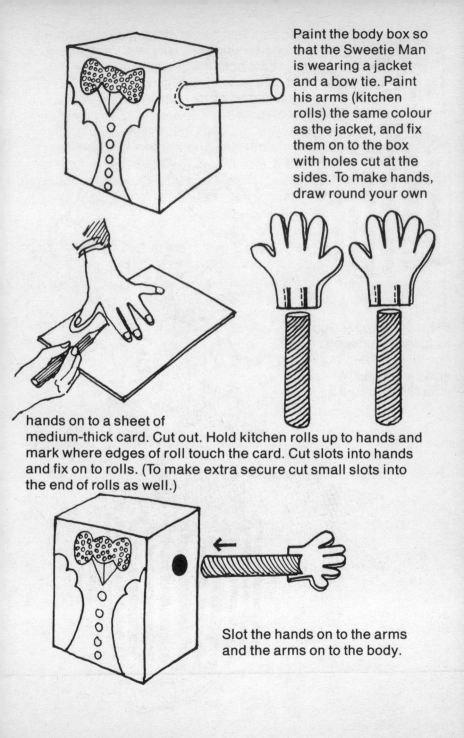

Paint the body box so that the Sweetie Man is wearing a jacket and a bow tie. Paint his arms (kitchen rolls) the same colour as the jacket, and fix them on to the box with holes cut at the sides. To make hands, draw round your own hands on to a sheet of medium-thick card. Cut out. Hold kitchen rolls up to hands and mark where edges of roll touch the card. Cut slots into hands and fix on to rolls. (To make extra secure cut small slots into the end of rolls as well.)

Slot the hands on to the arms and the arms on to the body.

Take smallest box to make the waist. Paint on a belt round centre of box. Paint above belt same colour as jacket and below the belt to look like top of trousers. Trousers box could be stripy. Continue sripes on to waist box.

Cut two big floppy feet out of medium-thick card and paint on brown boots.

Build Sweetie Man up by tucking feet under trousers box, then adding waist, body arms and head. What an impressive figure he is!